Cecilia Minden-Cupp, Ph.D.
Reading Specialist

by Bob Woods

Gareth Stevens Publishing
A WORLD ALMANAC EDUCATION GROUP COMPANY

Please visit our web site at: www.garethstevens.com
For a free color catalog describing Gareth Stevens Publishing's
list of high-quality books and multimedia programs,
call 1-800-542-2595 (USA) or 1-800-387-3178 (Canada).
Gareth Stevens Publishing's fax: (414) 332-3567.

Library of Congress Cataloging-in-Publication Data

Woods, Bob.
    In-line skating / by Bob Woods.
      p. cm. — (Extreme sports: an imagination library series)
    Summary: Briefly describes the equipment, techniques, and various locations involved in
in-line skating.
    Includes bibliographical references and index.
    ISBN 0-8368-3722-3 (lib. bdg.)
    1. In-line skating—Juvenile literature. [1. In-line skating.] I. Title. II. Extreme sports
(Milwaukee, Wis.)
GV859.73.W66   2003
796.21—dc21   2003042803

First published in 2004 by
Gareth Stevens Publishing
A World Almanac Education Group Company
330 West Olive Street, Suite 100
Milwaukee, WI 53212 USA

Text: Bob Woods
Cover design and page layout: Tammy Gruenewald
Series editor: Carol Ryback
Manuscript and photo research: Shoreline Publishing Group LLC

Photo credits: Cover, pp. 5, 7, 11, 13, 15 © Sports Gallery/Al Messerschmidt; p. 9
© Duomo/CORBIS; p. 17 © Tom Stewart/CORBIS; p. 19 © AP/Wide World Photos;
p. 21 © Paul Barton/CORBIS

Printed in the United States of America

1 2 3 4 5 6 7 8 9 07 06 05 04 03

Cover: In-line skates move you on the ground,
but this high-flying girl shows that in-line skates
also help you soar!

TABLE OF CONTENTS

Words that appear in the glossary are printed in **boldface** type the first time they occur in the text.

GET IN-LINE!

In-line skating became popular during the 1980s thanks to a company called Rollerblade®. Some people call this sport rollerblading, but the correct term is in-line skating.

In-line skates have four wheels in a straight line, making them look a little like ice skates.

Millions of people of all ages enjoy in-line skating. They skate for fun and exercise near their homes, at indoor and outdoor rinks, or on parks and trails.

Learn how to in-line skate and you can play in-line (roller) hockey or roller basketball. You could also compete in speedskating races!

Experienced skaters can do thrilling tricks. They "catch air" taking off from a U-shaped ramp called a **half-pipe**.

ALL GEARED UP

In-line skates come in many different models. Their cost ranges from $35 to $1,000. The price depends upon the type of boot, the brakes, and the quality of the wheels.

In-line boots should fit snugly around your feet and ankles. Skates have brakes at either the toe or the heel. Wheels come in different sizes and are made from a hard plastic called **urethane**. The wheels roll on **ball bearings**, which are inside the centers, or hubs, of the wheels.

Every in-line skater — from beginner to extreme professional — should always wear a properly fitting helmet, knee pads, elbow pads, and wrist guards.

Wrist guards protect skaters' hands, wrists, and forearms. Knee and elbow pads and a helmet also help prevent injuries.

LET THE GOOD TIMES ROLL

The best way to learn how to in-line skate is to take it slowly. Learn how to balance and glide on your skates. Don't let others pressure you into going fast or trying tricks.

Once you get comfortable, you can work on some advanced moves. Advanced moves include turning around, doing **crossovers**, and skating backwards. Practice on a wide, flat surface. Wear your helmet and elbow, wrist, and knee pads.

Don't be surprised if you stumble and fall every now and then. Everybody falls when learning. Before you know it, you'll be a smooth skater, too.

Most brands of in-line skates are available in sporting goods stores or wherever athletic shoes are sold.

RIDING THE RAILS

In-line skaters are always looking for thrills. Some extreme athletes skate backwards very fast, make 360-degree turns in the air, jump off ramps, and "bash" (skate) down steps without falling!

Extreme skaters — wearing protective helmets and pads, of course — also love to jump up and slide along railings.

Some rail-sliders remove one wheel from their skates or have a **grind plate** between wheels. They slide on the grind plate or the wheel frame, but not on the wheels themselves. However you do it, keeping your balance is the trickiest part.

Many extreme skaters like to perform or invent tricks, such as 360s, sliding on one skate, and sliding backwards. They might grind on the edge of a pipe, a railing, or a bench.

HEAD OVER WHEELS

You can get airborne with in-line skates, but watch out for those landings — and put your helmet on tight before takeoff!

Use a **quarter-pipe** or half-pipe ramp for your runway. Start out flying low. Once you're in the air, you can do different tricks.

A basic **grab** is a good move to try first. When you catch air, tuck your knees toward your chest. Swing your skates up. Point one arm toward the ground. With your other hand, reach for the wheels of the top skate. Next time, grab the wheels of your lower skate while you're airborne.

Practice closer to the ground before attempting high-flying stunts. Work out your move on a trampoline first. Ask a friend, parent, or trainer to **spot** you.

GO "VERT" IN A PIPE

Extreme in-line skaters do tricks in quarter-pipes and half-pipes. The walls of these pipes go straight up, or vertical — **"vert"** to skaters. You can learn to go "vert," too.

Begin by rolling back and forth in the curved portion of the pipe. Bend your knees on the way down to pick up speed. Swing up a little higher each time. Pretend your body is a **pendulum**.

When you swing close to the lip, grab it — and pull yourself to the top edge of the pipe. Then turn around and drop back in for an extreme ride.

You can do lots of tricks once you get good at ramp skating. This competitor at the Gravity Games is doing a perfect grab in midair. Notice how his knees are pulled up tight and together.

HOCKEY ON A ROLL

You can wear your regular in-line skates for roller hockey. You can also use regular ice-hockey sticks and pucks. Or you can buy special roller-hockey skates and other in-line hockey gear. Roller-hockey sticks have wooden handles and plastic blades.

Some roller-hockey players **rocker** the wheels on their skates for tighter turning. They lower the two center wheels to create a curved wheel alignment.

Extreme roller-hockey players wear a helmet, elbow pads, wrist guards, knee and shin guards, gloves, shoulder pads, and even a mouth guard. Make sure you wear your safety gear, too!

You don't need ice for roller hockey. Just play it in your driveway with a few of your friends. You can also join a roller-hockey league.

SPEED DEMONS

Speedskating is for very experienced, extreme in-line skaters. Some athletes use speed skating as a tough — but excellent — workout. Other speed skaters compete in individual or team races.

USA Roller Skating holds indoor and outdoor championship races every year. Packs of competitors compete on road courses or **banked** oval tracks.

In-line speed skates usually have five wheels instead of four. In-line speed-skating boots are shaped differently, too. The boots stop at the ankle. And like a racing bicycle, in-line speed skates usually don't have brakes.

Short-track in-line speedskating is a fast and furious worldwide sport. Don't be surprised to see in-line short-track speedskating at future Olympic Games.

HAPPY TRAILS TO YOU

The best thing about in-line skating is that all you need is your gear and a hard surface. A driveway, sidewalk, or your school's blacktopped playground are perfect for in-line skating.

You can also share paved hiking trails in parks and forests with walkers, joggers, bicyclists, and skateboarders. Remember to respect other people using the path. Stay to the right, and call out before you pass someone.

So grab your helmet, safety pads, and those in-line skates — and get in-line!

No matter how you choose to enjoy in-line skating, it's sure to put a smile on your face. Ask your friends and family to skate with you.

MORE TO READ AND VIEW

Books (Nonfiction)   *Aggressive In-Line Skating. Extreme Sports* (series).
    Anne T. McKenna (Capstone)
Downhill In-Line Skating. Extreme Sports (series).
    Nick Cook (Capstone)
Extreme In-Line Skating Moves. Behind the Moves (series).
    Danny Parr (Capstone)
For the Love of Inline Skating. For the Love of Sports (series).
    Rennay Craats (Weigl)
In-Line Skating. Action Sports (series). Joe Herran (Chelsea House)
In-Line Skating. Extreme Sports (series). Ben Roberts (Barrons)
In-Line Skating in Action. Sports in Action (series).
    John Crossingham (Crabtree)
In-Line Skating. Radical Sports (series). Bernie Blackall (Heinemann)

Books (Fiction)   *In-line Skater: Cris Must Decide: Half-Pipe or Hockey Rink?*
    Matt Christopher (Little, Brown & Company)
Out of Line. X Games Xtreme Mysteries, No. 6 (series).
    Laban Carrick Hill (Hyperion)
Wait, Skates! Rookie Reader, Level C (series).
    Mildred D. Johnson (Children's Press)

Videos   *Desmond's In-line Skating.* (Tapeworm)
In-Line Skating Workout Video. (Lamb)
Let's Roll: In-line Skating. (Tapeworm)

WEB SITES

Web sites change frequently, but we believe the following web sites are going to last. You can also use good search engines, such as **Yahooligans! (www.yahooligans.com)** or **Google (www.google.com)** to find more information about in-line skating. Some keywords that will help you are: *Anthony Lobello, extreme sports, in-line skating (also inline skating), and skating safety.*

www.cbc4kids.cbc.ca/general/whatsnew/ sport-of-the-month/april99/default.html
CBC 4 Kids gives the history of in-line skating, how to get started with this extreme sport, and the best ways to brake well and fall gracefully.

www.nysgtsc.state.ny.us/kid-bike.htm
Be safe when you skate! Check this page for a look at the right gear to wear, the importance of helmets, and the meaning of several traffic signs.

www.iisa.org/kids/
The International In-line Skating Association provides ideas for cool skating tricks and activities for kids of all ages. It also provides tips on how to get an area in your town designated just for in-line skating.

www.bam.gov/whiz_kids/expert/ inline_skating.htm
Whiz Kids features an article on professional in-line skater Anthony Lobello.

www.bam.gov/survival/play_ inline_skating.htm
Bam! offers survival skills that every in-line skater should know, such as where to skate and why it's so important to always wear a helmet.

www.rollerskatingmuseum.com/ serv02.htm
This National Museum of Roller Skating page covers the history of this extreme sport and includes a time line of in-line skating events.

www.thesportsauthority.com/
Click on in-line skating under the sport column for tips on how to buy in-line skating safety equipment.

web.skatefaq.com:81/glossary.html
Impress your friends with your knowledge of in-line skating terms. Contains links to general in-line information, techniques, skating locations, and tutorials.

GLOSSARY

You can find these words on the pages listed. Reading a word in a sentence helps you understand it even better.

ball bearings — steel balls packed inside a wheel that help it roll more easily. 6

banked — having curved walls or sides. 18

crossovers — crossing one foot in front of the other, over and over as you skate. 8

grab — touching the bottom of one of your skates while in the air. 12, 14

grind plate — a plate on the bottom of an in-line skate that helps you slide. 10

half-pipe — a U-shaped ramp. 4, 12, 14

pendulum — a device that swings back and forth with a very regular motion. 14

quarter-pipe — a shallow, curved ramp. 12, 14

rocker — to change the position of your in-line skate's wheels to form a curve. 16

short-track — a speedskating race (both in-line and ice) that uses a 33-yard- (30-meter-) long track. The short-track race length is about four times shorter than the length of a regular skating race. 18

spot — to watch and be ready to assist another athlete as he or she practices. 12

urethane (YOUR-a-thane) — a hard plastic used for making in-line skate wheels. 6

vert — short for vertical, or straight up. 14

INDEX

.